Are you a teacher?

Alessandra Borg

Presentation by *BookLeaf Publishing*

Web: www.bookleafpub.com

E-mail: info@bookleafpub.com

ISBN: 9789395755047

First edition 2022

DEDICATION

This collection of poems is dedicated to anyone I've ever taught, who has taught me, or who has asked me, "Are you a teacher?" at least once.

PREFACE

If you have the honour of being acquainted with a teacher, perhaps a friend, a brother, a daughter, or someone you play footy with on the weekends, I am sure you have heard more stories about school than you could possibly want. This is certainly the experience of my family who frequently ask me, somewhat sarcastically, "Are you a teacher?" after my endless anecdotes that I (and apparently only I) thought were funny or interesting. So here is a book of poems on the topic, written so that I could release some of my thoughts and feelings for people perhaps a little more interested in school life than those who currently hear my stories. Please note that, while inspired by real events, none of the poems in this collection are entirely factual and any similarities to real people or events is unintentional.

First day of school

First day of school
Get in early
No students here yet
Organise desk
Where's my pen?
No, not that one
Yes, the black one
Write my name
In my new diary
Find my timetable
In my pigeon-hole
Morning briefing
In the staff room
Back to the office
Ball hits window
Students are here now
Playing downball
Check my emails
No new messages
Did my planning
Over the holidays
Load my welcome slides
Stack my books
Fresh set of whiteboard markers
Time to go to class
There goes the bell

Students to their lockers
Teachers to their classrooms
Ready, set, go!

Marking the roll

No one could know all the ways
(It would take them days)
To spell each and every single name
Even when they are pronounced the same
Like Sara with no 'H'
And Khloe with a 'K'
Amelia, Emilia, Emily, and Amelie;
Luca, Luka, Luke, and Lucas.

Each year I meet new variations
Thanks to parents' cool creations
And try my best to say them right
But though I try with all my might
There's Louis pronounced like Lewis
And silent letters too
Eva, Evie, Eve, and Yves;
Ava, Avery, Aalvyn, and Niamh.

Ridiculous that those last two lines rhyme
But wonderful to live in such a time
As now when all the cultures merge
And we experience a surge
In names like Sumaya,
Hieu, Aryan, and Kyri
Giacomo, Omar, Christos, and Asha;

Femke, Andrej, Nikolaus, and Hana.

So let's embrace this little change
And celebrate the endless range
Of all our students' lovely names.

The rules

Good morning students!
5, 4, 3, 2, 1...
Quiet please!
Don't talk when I'm talking!
Don't put your feet on the desk!
Keep your hands to yourself.
Don't copy his work!
Don't draw on her work!
Write your name on your book.
Don't forget to do your homework!
Don't cheat off someone else's!
Bring your equipment to class.
Don't lose your textbook!
Don't eat food in class!
Turn around and face the front.
Don't write on the desks!
Don't swear or make inappropriate comments!
Put your gum in the bin.
Don't bring your phone to class!
Don't wear the wrong coloured socks!
Come to class on time.
Don't leave this until the last minute!
Don't say "I can't"!
Just give it a go.
Don't say that about yourself!

Don't say that about your friend!
Be kind to each other.
Don't worry!
Don't be upset!
You've given it your best effort.
Don't be scared of making mistakes!
Don't give up when you get it wrong!
You're learning.

10 students in every class

1. The class clown
2. The class clown's very quiet best friend
3. The kid that rolls their eyes at the class clown
4. The kid that tells the class clown to shut up
5. The straight A student
6. The student who would get straight As if they paid attention
7. The student who needs to go to the bathroom
8. The student who is currently in the bathroom that the other student who needs to go has to wait for to come back before they can go
9. The kid that asks too many questions
10. No-name... sorry, I don't know who you are, you forgot to write your name on the test

Recess

End of lesson bell
Students run, eat, laugh and play.
Hope no one gets hurt!

Yard duty is like a box of chocolates

Yard duty is like a box of chocolates:
Yard duty can be cold, wet, and miserable,
Yard duty can be sunny, warm, and joyous.
You never know what you're going to get!

Yard duty is like a box of chocolates:
Yard duty includes lizards, dirt, and bees' nests,
Yard duty includes footballs, books, and music.
You never know what you're going to get!

Yard duty is like a box of chocolates:
Yard duty causes fights, tears, and breaking
school rules,
Yard duty causes imagination, laughter, and
making new friends.
You never know what you're going to get!

Band session

Squawks and squeaks...
Make little tweaks!
We're starting soon,
so play in tune.
Breathe together!
Shoes of leather
tap the beat.
Play the repeat!
Sweet melodies
make memories,
here, with our friends.
Success depends
on co-operation.
Use your imagination!
Count to four!
Now, let's explore...
Dynamics and articulation
should be your main preoccupation:
How soft or loud?
Play nice and proud!
And long or short?
You great cohort!
Read your chart!
All be a part
of the joy we share

when we all care
enough to spend
our long day's end
making organised sound
and mucking around.
May you never be too sick
to make beautiful music.

Chronicle post

This student has been very efficient in class this week.
This student has shown resilient behaviour in the classroom.
This student has made an excellent start on their assignment.
This student has arrived late to class every day this week.
This student has come top of the class in our revision trivia quiz.
This student has used their mobile phone during class.
This student has been caught chewing gum.
This student has demonstrated a solid understanding of our new topic.

I was really impressed by the amount of work completed.
I was proud of them for taking on a challenge.
I was pleased to see how focused they were.
I was disappointed by their lack of organisation.
I was blown away by how well they remembered the content.

I was thoroughly unimpressed by their disregard
of school rules.
I was happy they admitted they were doing the
wrong thing.
I was surprised at how much they retained after
such a short time.

This is a testament to their diligence in class.
This is a testament to their persistence.
This is a testament to their determination and
effort.
This is a testament to their carelessness about
school.
This is a testament to their consistent work
habits and study skills.
This is a testament to their rebellious attitude
towards authority figures.
This is a testament to their honesty and
admirable character.
This is a testament to their willingness to learn.

I hope this work ethic continues throughout the
term.
I hope this attitude towards learning will stay
with them.
I hope this hard work early on will pay off in the
final product.
I hope this tardiness will not be an ongoing
issue.

I hope this helps them realise that they can do anything they set their mind to.
I hope this does not happen again.
I hope this will remind them to do the right thing in future.
I hope this is only the beginning of a successful year.

Did we need that meeting?

After school meetings
that could have been an email
really need to stop.

School holidays

Forty weeks of school
Would make any teacher drool
As each student becomes a ghoul
If not for a certain tool
That's really rather cool
It's time spent by the pool
Without a single rule
The educator's jewel
To skip them would be cruel
School holidays!

At the end of every term
My brain becomes a worm
And yes I can confirm
That everyone would squirm
And wish they caught some germ
If only to affirm
Or get another perm
Lay on their mattress firm
Dream they're standing on a berm
School holidays!

For each and every day
From June right through to May
The shining little ray

Apart from the obvious pay
Breaking through the grey
And making us shout 'Yay!'
A well-earned holiday
To settle in the hay
And hear the horses neigh
School holidays!

In the quiet of a test

You've learned all you can
And I know you've all studied
We've followed the plan
Now you shouldn't be worried
Just focus and show
All that you know
In the quiet of a test

You've listened and heard
But your classmates are distracting
Please don't say another word
Now is not the time for acting
Just focus and show
All that you know
In the quiet of a test

You've done all you could
Make sure you've checked it over
Move paper over wood
You're bright as a supernova
Just focus and show
All that you know
In the quiet of a test

Emails from absent students

They start off with a greeting:
Hi miss, hi sir, good morning
Hope you're well!

Then onto their excuses:
I don't mean to be a nuisance...
I've been sick!

A question or request:
I want to do my best...
What did I miss?

And then ask for an extension:
So as not to get detention...
Can I have an extra week?

Signing off with song and dance:
Thank you in advance!
Warm regards, yours sincerely

Are you a teacher?

Oh, what else is there to say
After a long and stressful day?
My head so full of anecdotes
Fun stories, bizarre quotes,
I can't help it, though I try,
To avoid my friends all cry,
"Are you a teacher?"

Oh, how else could I begin
With any, dare I say, chagrin?
I love and live my job,
So yes I hate to hear the mob,
"Are you a teacher?"

Oh, when else am I allowed
To admit that I am proud?
My students are hilarious,
If at times a bit nefarious...
Yes, I'm a teacher!

Parent teacher interviews in 7 minutes

Minute 1: Figuring out who's next in line. Is it us? Is it them? Dreaded line cutters. Take a seat!

Minute 2: Big smiles, how's it going? Nice to meet you! Likewise. Checking notes to remember names.

Minute 3: Your child is an absolute delight and if I had a class full of students like them I would be endlessly happy!

Minute 4: Awkward pause. Asked the student how they feel about my subject. Alright I guess. Parents nudge them. Student's thinking.

Minute 5: Student finally asks a question, prompted by mum. Oh yeah! What else can I do for more extension? I'm so glad you asked.

Minute 6: Assigning tasks I know the student won't complete, as much as mum will try to make them. It's for your own good! You'll realise when you're older.

Minute 7: Time to say goodbye. Got to run on time. Next parents are already waiting. See you next time!

Professional development

23

Annual tasks due.
How long can PD go for?
20. Minutes? Hours.

40 weeks of school

Every faculty has its week
Designed to make the year less bleak.
With each one we might just tweak
Our students' mojo so to speak,
Because induce smiles cheek to cheek
These celebrations; they're the peak.

Performing Arts week gives a chance
To students who just love to prance.
They pass their time with song and dance,
Despite their classmate's sideways glance.
So pretty please don't look askance,
Or else beware a dramatic lance!

Health and PE week I must admit
Inspires us all to never quit.
Staff v students games are always a hit,
Especially with the scoreboard lit.
For those less agile an oven mitt
Is used to cook food that keeps us fit.

We never see the library look
Like such a full and thriving nook,
But Book Week is all that it took

To turn our hearts towards a book!
And then the walls quite clearly shook
With our applause for Captain Hook.

Maths Week causes quite a stir,
Festivities just like decimals recur.
It would take more than pi to deter,
Ms P's students from throwing a pie right at her!
Honestly, the whole week is one big blur,
Except for whoever wins Countdown, well dur!

Who could forget the unmistakable tang
That Science Week brings going off with a
bang?
So many explosions you'd think there's a gang
All of the students just know where to hang,
To join competitions, and lose them, oh dang!
Somebody even brought in a real fang!

With all of these weeks at every school,
It's easy to see why learning is cool.
And yet, though they are a powerful tool,
Bringing lunches and prizes to make students
drool,
It's important to remember one simple rule:
You must know what week it is, don't be a fool!

Ode to remote learning

Though it made us sad,
Remote learning wasn't bad!
Oh such fun we had.

No morning commute,
The peace you cannot refute:
Students left on mute.

We were all at home,
Free to chat, eat, play and roam
Our restricted dome.

Lots of online shops
Buying toys and shoes and tops
Spending never stops.

Learning via Zoom,
No impending sense of doom
From my own bedroom.

10 foods sold in all school canteens

1. Sausage rolls, saucy and scrumptious, sizzling inside soft plastic sleeves
2. Vegetarian and vegan options loaded with green veggies like spinach and cabbage
3. Pizza topped with pepperoni, piping hot, and pressed to perfection
4. Luscious lasagne you long for and love
5. Chicken nuggets you call nuggies, golden nuggets, fried to a crisp
6. Nachos that are really just corn chips and cheese melted over them with maybe a dollop of salsa
7. Muffins so magically soft just like clouds, some warm and cinnamony or gooey and chocolatey
8. Ice-cream, you scream, we all scream for ice-cream
9. Icy poles as cold as the North Pole
10. Coffee for teachers and the older kids who are studying, avoid at all costs for it means you're working hard!

I love my job

I love my job
Like corn on the cob
Or dogs in the park
Very excitedly bark
Each day is unique
My interest will pique
Yes I love what I do
Just so much I tell you
Only teachers could know
But how good it is though

Why I hate taking days off

Taking a day off
Is more trouble than it's worth.
Ask any teacher.

The last day of school

Last day of school
Finish early
Most students stayed home
Pack up desk
I found my pen!
No, not that one
Yes, my best one
Shred the pages
Of my old diary
Toss my timetable
Empty pigeon-hole
Morning tea break
In the staff room
Back to the office
Pack my bags up
Students all gone now
It's a ghost town
Check my emails
No new messages
I'll do my planning
Over the holidays
Close my lesson slides
Shelve my books
Throw out used whiteboard markers
Time to go home

There goes the bell
Students to their parents' cars
Teachers to their after parties
Going, going, gone.

www.ingramcontent.com/pod-product-compliance
Lightning Source LLC
LaVergne TN
LVHW010948200726
843509LV00013B/2320